Learning With Shapes
MILK
to Grow On

by

Doris Cambruzzi and Claire Thornton

illustrations by Lorraine Arthur

STANDARD PUBLISHING
Cincinnati, Ohio   3610

This is my book.

My name is _____.

Library of Congress Catalog Card Number 86-060740
ISBN 0-87403-130-3

© 1986, The STANDARD PUBLISHING Company
Division of STANDEX INTERNATIONAL Corporation
Printed in U.S.A.

Dear Parent:

God, our loving Father, has entrusted our children to us, to guide and direct in both spiritual and bodily growth here on earth. This book is designed to help your children become familiar with good nutrition so that they will eat the correct foods for a healthy body.

Nutrition pertains to what we eat and how our bodies use it. Essential nutrients must be obtained from the foods we eat. Protein, carbohydrates, fat, vitamins, minerals, and water are the six classes of essential nutrients we obtain from our diets.

Whether we eat at home or we eat out, we are faced with important food choices. Children's needs change with age. One set of rules simply cannot apply to everyone. There is a practical guide to good nutrition, which translates the technical knowledge of nutrition into a plan for everyday eating. This guide, "The Four Food Groups," provides the kind and quantity of food necessary for a balanced diet. The Four Food Groups are Fruit-Vegetable Group, Meat Group, Milk Group, and Bread-Cereal Group.

A key to good health is to eat a variety of foods from each of the four food groups every day and get proper rest and exercise. It is very important to start your young children with good health habits.

Why do some people accept some foods and reject others? A primary factor in food acceptance seems to be the training of the young child in familiarity with a wide variety of foods. This training should be started at an early age, supported both in the home and by effective educational experiences..

Coauthor Doris Cambruzzi conducted a study on this subject and found that education, in addition to the provision of food, was an important factor in the vegetable consumption practices of children. The pattern of eating established during early childhood is believed to affect food choice and, to some extent, nutritional status throughout life.

This book is a learning aid to help your child become familiar with foods from the Milk Group and to understand the correct portion that is needed by the body, which is the key to weight control throughout life. The illustrations of milk and milk products contained in this book will help children identify them, and the recipes are easy and fun.

—Doris Cambruzzi
—Claire Thornton

EAT A VARIETY OF FOODS FROM

FRUIT-VEGETABLE GROUP

Eat 4 or more servings each day from the Vegetable-Fruit Group. Foods in this group supply most of our daily need for vitamin C and vitamin A. Fiber is present in all fruits and vegetables, especially in the skins.

One serving from the
Fruit-Vegetable Group
= ½ cup of a fruit or vegetable, or a portion as ordinarily served, such as 1 medium banana

MEAT GROUP

Eat 2 or more servings daily of foods from the Meat Group. Foods in this group supply protein and iron and they are a good source of the B vitamins.

One serving from the
Meat Group
= 2 or 3 ounces of cooked meat, poultry or fish
= 2 eggs
= 1 cup of dry beans, peas, or lentils
= 4 tablespoons of peanut butter

THE FOUR FOOD GROUPS!

BREAD-CEREAL GROUP

Eat 4 or more servings each day from the Bread-Cereal Group. Foods in this group supply many of the vitamins in the B complex, iron, carbohydrates and limited amounts of protein. Fiber is present in whole grains.

One serving from the
Bread-Cereal Group

= 1 slice of bread
= 1 ounce of ready-to-eat cereal
= ½ to ¾ cup of cooked cereal macaroni, rice, grits, or spaghetti

MILK GROUP

Turn the page and have fun with the Milk Group.

God made us, and God made the food we eat. God made the land and the sea, the sun and the moon, the rain and the air around us, and all the animals and plants for us to enjoy.

Milk and milk products are some of the foods that God gave us to eat. They taste good and are good for us.

God wants us to have healthy bodies and to take good care of our bodies. When we eat the right foods, we grow and feel good; and when we feel good, we can serve Him better.

This book tells you about milk and milk products and gives you some recipes so that you can enjoy drinking and eating them in different ways. You will also learn to identify the many shapes in our world.

Have fun eating foods from the Milk Group; they will help you stay healthy!

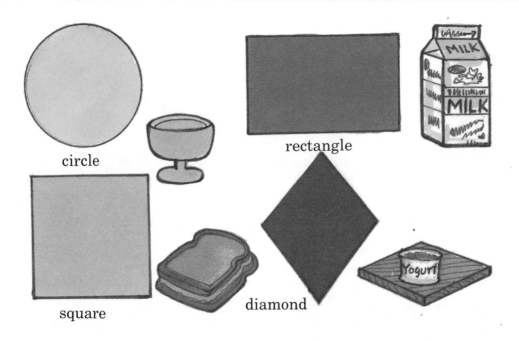

circle

rectangle

square

diamond

The Milk Group

The Milk Group is a major source of the mineral called calcium.

It also contains vitamin B_2, phosphorous, and some protein.

When we drink "fortified milk," it provides us with vitamins A and D.

Vitamin D helps our bodies use calcium.

Why Calcium Is Good for Us

Calcium helps children's bones and teeth to grow and be strong.

We need calcium every day because our bones are being rebuilt throughout our lives.

Calcium helps our blood to clot if we cut ourselves.

Our muscles need calcium when we exercise, run, and play.

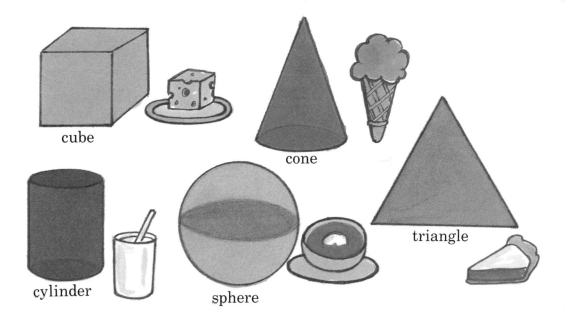

cube

cone

cylinder

sphere

triangle

Servings From the Milk Group

One serving = 1 cup (8 ounces) of milk, whole, lowfat, or skim

Children under 9 need 2 to 3 servings daily.
Children 9 to 12 need 3 or more servings daily.
Teenagers need 4 or more servings daily.
Adults need 2 or more servings daily.

Lowfat and skim milk products have the same amount of calcium as whole milk, but not as many calories.

What Equals One Serving of Calcium?

One serving of calcium

= 1 cup (8 ounces) of milk
= 1 ounce of yellow or white cheese
= 1¾ cups of ice cream
= 2 cups of cottage cheese
= 1 cup (8 ounces) of yogurt

1 cup (8 ounces) of milk

1 ounce of yellow or white cheese

1¾ cups of ice cream

2 cups of cottage cheese

1 cup (8 ounces) of yogurt

CIRCLE

Custard is a good way
to get milk in your diet.

Baked Custard

2 eggs
¼ cup sugar
¼ teaspoon salt
2 cups milk, scalded
½ teaspoon vanilla
Nutmeg for flavoring

Heat oven to 350 degrees.

Beat eggs, sugar, and salt together slightly to mix.

Scald milk in heavy pan over high heat until bubbles form around the edge.

Stir scalded milk into egg mixture.

Add vanilla.

Pour into 6 custard cups or a 1½ quart baking dish and set in a pan of hot water (1 inch up on cups or baking dish).

Sprinkle on nutmeg.

Bake 35 to 45 minutes, or until a knife inserted 1 inch from the edge comes out clean.

Makes 6 servings.

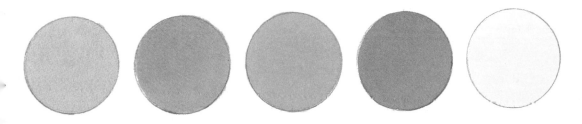

RECTANGLE

Pudding is made with milk,
so it gives our bodies calcium.

Pudding Cupcakes

1 package cake mix
1 package instant pudding mix
Powdered sugar for decoration

Follow the directions on the box of cake mix to make cupcakes.

Put cupcake papers in muffin tin.

Pour batter into each cupcake paper until it is half full.

Bake as directed on package.

Remove cupcakes and cool.

Cut the top off of each cupcake.

Take a spoon and hollow out the center of each cupcake.

Make pudding mix according to the directions on the package.

Pour into the center of each cupcake.

Put the top back on.

Sprinkle with powdered sugar and eat.

Store leftovers in the refrigerator.

SQUARE

Cheese comes from milk.

Grilled Cheese Sandwich

2 slices of cheese
4 slices of bread
Butter or margarine

Melt 1 teaspoon of butter or margarine in a skillet on low heat.

Butter 4 slices of bread on only one side.

Place two slices of bread in the pan, buttered side down.

Put a slice of cheese on each piece of bread.

Place the other slices of bread on top, buttered sides up.

Brown the sandwiches on one side and then turn them over with a spatula.

When both sides of the sandwiches are brown, serve them on plates with tomato slices and pickles.

Makes 2 servings.

Tip: To keep cheese from getting tough, cook for only a short time at a low temperature.

DIAMOND

Yogurt is made from milk.

Yogurt Dip With Fresh Fruit

1 container (8 ounces) of vanilla yogurt
Apple slices
Pear slices
Orange sections
Whole strawberries
Melon slices

Spoon yogurt into a small bowl and arrange fruit slices around it for dipping.

Note: Plain yogurt mixed with one tablespoon of honey may be used instead of vanilla yogurt.

CUBE

Cheese makes a good snack
because it gives us
calcium and protein.

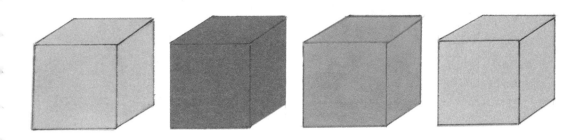

Cheese Kabobs

4 one-inch cheese cubes, yellow or white
2 small cherry tomatoes
1 cooked hot dog, cut into 4 pieces
1 dill pickle, cut into 4 pieces
2 bamboo skewers or long toothpicks

Stick a cube of cheese, a cherry tomato, a piece of hot dog, and a piece of pickle, then another tomato, piece of cheese, hot dog, and pickle on each skewer.

Serve on a party plate.

Makes 2 servings.

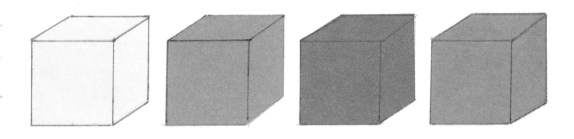

CONE

Ice cream is made from milk and cream.

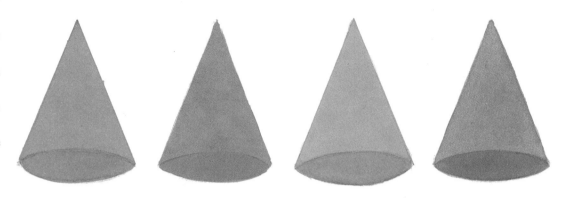

Upside-Down Ice-Cream Cone Clowns

2 pointed cones
2 large round cookies
Ice cream
Gum drops, small chocolate candies, and cinnamon
  drops for decoration
Can of instant whipped cream

Place one scoop of ice cream in each cone.

Put a cookie on top of each scoop of ice cream, then turn upside-down on a plate.

Make a face on each scoop of the ice cream using pieces of candy for the eyes, nose, and mouth.

Squirt a ruffle of whipped cream around the edge of each cookie.

Eat right away, or freeze until ready to serve.

Serves 2, but you can make as many as you need.

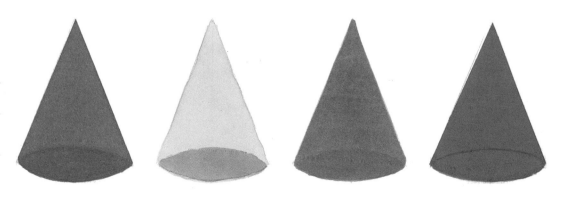

CYLINDER

Drinks made with milk
are good for you at mealtime
or in-between meals.

Milky Nutra-Shake

½ cup skim milk
¼ banana
3 tablespoons orange juice concentrate
7 ice cubes

Put ingredients in a blender and whip until smooth.
Pour into a tall glass and serve.
Makes 1 ¾ cups.

Note: Other fruits such as strawberries can be used instead of bananas.

SPHERE

Cottage cheese is made from milk.

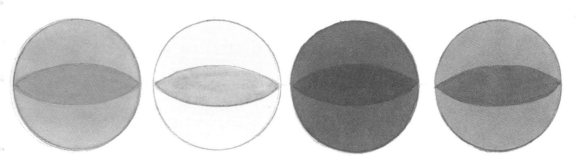

Soup With a Scoop

1 can cream of tomato soup
Milk
2 scoops of cottage cheese

Make cream of tomato soup according to the directions on the can using milk.

Pour into 2 bowls.

Place a scoop of cottage cheese on top of the soup in the center of each bowl.

Serve with crackers.

Makes 2 large servings.

Cream soups are another good way to eat the daily servings of milk which we need to keep our bodies healthy.

Cream pie fillings are made with milk.

TRIANGLE

Easy Chocolate Cream Pie

1 large package of instant chocolate pudding and pie
  filling
1 graham cracker pie crust, ready-made
Milk
Can of instant whipped cream

Make the pie filling according to directions on the package using milk.

Pour the chocolate filling into the graham cracker crust.

Chill in the refrigerator for at least 1 hour.

Squirt whipped cream around the top of the pie to decorate.

Cut the pie into triangular pieces and serve.

Serves 6.

ALL

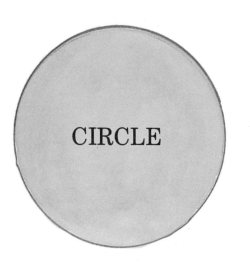

CIRCLE

RECTANGLE

SQUARE

DIAMOND

SHAPES

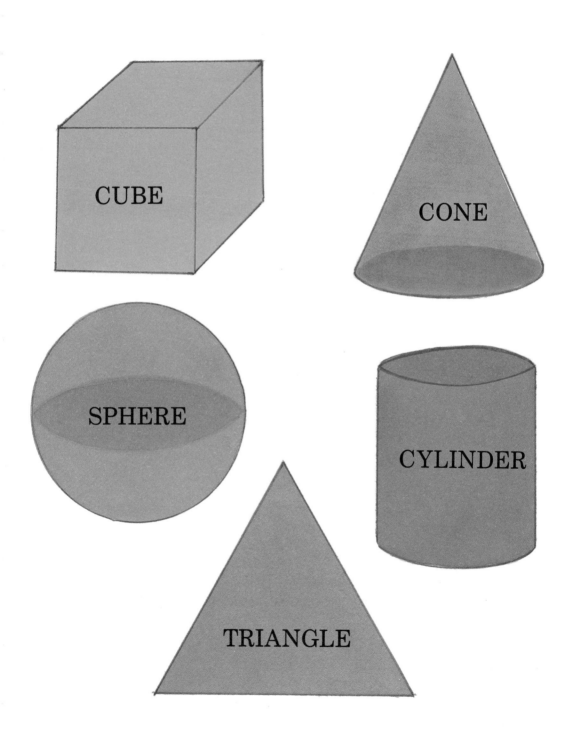

CUBE

CONE

SPHERE

CYLINDER

TRIANGLE

WHERE DOES MILK

Dairy farmers milk the cows with electric machines.

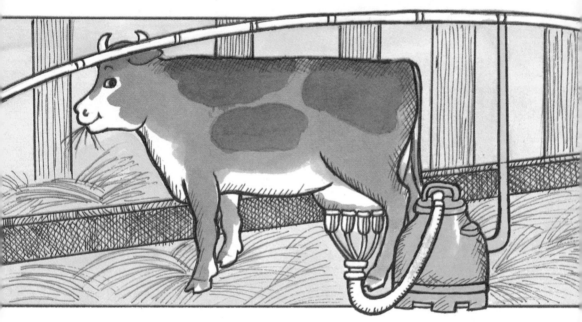

Refrigerated trucks take the milk to the dairy plant.

The milk is pasteurized by heating it to kill harmful bacteria.

Then the milk is put into bottles or cartons

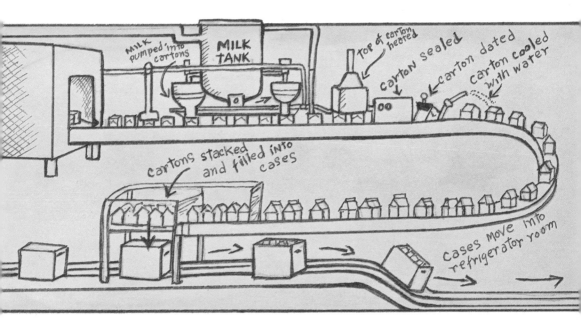

and delivered to the stores and supermarkets,

or to your home by the milkman.

We thank You, God, for milk to grow on. Amen.